# Real Estate Investing:

# How to double the value of your home for little - or even no money!

## By Gerald R. Walton

# Table of Contents

# Introduction

Increasing the value of your home should be on any real estate investor's radar. Whether it's your primary residence, or a home you've bought to flip, or the increasingly popular "live and flip" lifestyle - it's a no brainer, and an essential component to building huge wealth for you and your family.

The average American now spends 33% of their income on housing expenditures. So, by making smart decisions regarding real estate, you can cut that number in half. That represents real money in your pocket, not tiny gains made by skipping Starbucks or making your own packed lunch.

Gone are the days where people bought a home at 22 and proceeded to live in it for their entire lives. Now more than ever, re-sale price should be at the forefront of your mind when it comes to carrying out home renovations.

But, it's tough to know which renovations are worth it. Will you make your money back?

However, what 90% of amateur real estate investors don't know is that there are a ton of ways you can increase the value of your home for little money, or even FOR FREE!

It pays to get it right when it comes to renovations. So before you paint the living room hot pink, drop 10 large on a brand new steam room, or spend $5,000 on a full garden remodeling - take a look at these handy tips.

Beyond renovations, when it comes time to sell your home, there are a number of steps you can take to give yourself a huge advantage, and maximize your profits - even in a bad market!

I hope you learn a lot from this book, and I hope you make a lot of money with real estate going forward.

Finally, if you enjoyed reading this book - I'd really appreciate it if you left it a review on Amazon.

# 26 Ways to Increase Final Sale Price for Little or even No Money at all!

Use these low cost, and even free tips to add significant amounts to the final sale price of your home.

### Clean up outside

Studies have shown that litter outside can decrease your home value by up to 12%. This goes to show that even something tiny, and technically outside of your control - can negatively affect your home in a huge way.

### Get the garden in order

You've sorted out the front, now it's time to deal with the back. Grab those weeds and get them out of there as soon as possible. Fire up the hedge trimmer and keep everything neat and tidy. Even a $2 pot of heather by your front door can give a warm, welcoming appeal to any guest or home viewer.

## Ditch the novelty door knob

You never get a second chance to make a first impression, and that's no less true than in home buying and selling. I'm sure your love of cats or pumpkins is completely justified, but remember not everyone shares the same tastes. Neutral may be boring, but remember your door, mailbox and letterbox are among the first things people see when they come to view your home.

Homeowners have reported up to a 5% increase in offer just after changing from a novelty door knob or a more traditional one.

The same goes if you're stuck with a large, uninviting steel door. You can easily add wood grain to make it look nicer, and if you're looking for a cheaper option - just paint it.

Get some brand new stainless steel house numbers as well, at just $5-10 each they're well worth the investment.

The novelty doormat can go as well, "Welcome, bitches" and "Owner is shady, dogs are cool" may not be to everyone's taste...

## Upgrade your light fixtures

Another fairly cheap improvement is upgraded lighting, especially for your kitchen. Get rid of the dull, recessed lights in the kitchen and opt for an inexpensive - but nice looking chandelier instead. You can get some really great traditional and modern designs for as little as $100 online.

**Paint your way to profits**

A gallon of good quality paint costs around $25 on average. Once again, neutral colors work best and have the widest appeal, so maybe keep the military greens and cotton candy pinks on the shelf for another day.

If you're going to pick just one room to paint, make it the kitchen or living room - as these have a greater "first impression" appeal than the master bedroom.

One thing to note about kitchen colors is that white doesn't work. Design experts at Zillow Digs found that homes with all white kitchens sold for $1,400 less than equivalent ones with kitchens of over light hues.

If your budget allows for it, do an external repainting. Nothing says "I could lowball these guys" than an outdated external paintjob. So if your home is looking faded, painting is a great way to bring your value up to where it should be.

Remember to keep colors consistent with the rest of your neighborhood - no one wants to live in "the pink house".

**Pro tip:** If you go to Home Depot, Lowes, Ace Hardware or any other large home improvement store, you can often find near-full pots of paint for up to 50% off. This is known as the "oops" paint, where buyers have returned the pot after realising they didn't like the color. The best part is, you can often find these in multiple pots so if you have a large painting job you can save hundreds of dollars this way.

## Popcorn Ceilings

Remember when popcorn ceilings were in? Me neither - but many houses still have them. If yours suffers from this unfortunate affliction, get rid of them ASAP.

While this process is fairly labor intensive, it's also extremely cheap to sort out yourself. Make sure you completely cover all furniture before you begin.

## Putting in a pool will drown your home value

Everyone loves a pool right? Wrong.

Many low-maintenance types don't want to deal with the hassle of having to constantly maintain a pool year-round, especially in areas where it's not usable for all 12 months.

## If it's broke - definitely do fix it

You'd be surprised just how much minor (and cheap) cosmetic renovations can have a positive overall effect on your home value. Fixing broken roof tiles and cleaning the gutters are just two of the many things you can do in half a day which can easily increase home value by 1 or 2%. Remember, minor edges like this are what sets professionals apart from amateurs in the real estate market.

## Install a new showerhead

Remember the 5 star hotel experience you want to provide? Well all 5 star hotels have great showers, and particularly, great showerheads. This is a simple job you can do yourself and often involves nothing more than using pliers or a wrench to remove your old shower head then repeat the process in reverse for a new one.

Although luxury models can cost upwards of $1,000, you can get good mid-range rain style showerheads for as little as $200 at Home Depot.

## Bedrooms bring profits

Converting a bedroom into a home gym, studio or wine cellar may appeal to some, but to most buyers the more bedrooms the better.

This doubles down when you start installing semi-permanent items like specialist refrigerators and bookshelves that the new owner will have to spend money to gut and get rid of. So if you are going to convert one, with the view to moving out in a few years, ensure the features are easy to return to their natural state.

So remember this, if you have a three-bedroom house with a den, the only reason the den can't be considered a bedroom may be because it doesn't have a closet. If you add a closet to that room, you've now got a four-bedroom house - it's just that simple.

For the price of an Ikea closet, you can have an entire extra bedroom in your house.

## Garages are for cars

Following on from the bedroom conversion point. Garages converted to play rooms or home gyms are far less valuable to a garage to it used for its intended function - to store cars. Buyers want to keep their cars out of the rain and snow and have a space to store all their outdoor gear.

Note for my UK readers: The opposite is true across the pond. With the rise of off-street parking with larger driveways, 90% of British garages don't contain a car - so removing you garage and adding extra living space may well pay off. It costs around £10,000 to remove your garage and you can calculate your rough ROI by multiplying square footage gained by local price per square foot.

**Ask your realtor**

An often overlooked area - no one does this, and I really don't know why. Simply ask your realtor what kind of features people are looking for when they buy a house in your area, then add them. That way you don't have to try and predict what people will like, and more importantly won't have to rely on your own imagination.

**Kit out your kitchen**

You can absolutely do this on the cheap - so you don't need to go hunting for the marble catalogue anytime soon. Even basic cosmetic upgrades like replacing the faucets, cabinet door handles and lighting fixtures can have a dramatically positive effect.

If you can't afford to replace things, just give them a coat of paint - even this gives your kitchen an extra boost.

The kitchen is still very much the heart and soul of the home. It's where everyone congregates at parties and it's where most of that "accidental" family time (that people value the most) occurs - and more importantly, it's where buyers and realtors make a beeline for in houses they know will fetch a high price.

Little fixes like energy efficient lightbulbs, a nice floral centerpiece for a viewing can really put a potential buyer in a good mood, and drive up their own perceived value of the home.

Having cohesive appliances is another value booster.

You may have read the dishwasher bullet point in the Amazon description for this book. Well, here's the secret revealed by a customer service representative of a major manufacturer.

Many dishwasher panels are white on one side and black on the other. So if yours doesn't match, you may be able to just flip it around so it does!

All you have to do is unscrew two screws, slide out the panel and flip it around. Sure enough you have a black (or white) panel to match your other appliances.

## (Don't) Look down

I hate to break it to your but your floor is probably gross. Especially if it's more than 10 years old. Old, scruffy carpet isn't doing anyone any favors. Plus, flooring is one of the first thing buyers notice when they enter a property.

It's not a case of hardwood vs. carpet - it's a case of clean and new vs. dirty and old. No matter what kind of flooring you have, make sure it's clean. If you have a few hundred dollars spare I'd recommend getting your carpet deep cleaned by a pro.

Replacing the carpet is usually a poor investment as this is often one of the first improvements buyers make when purchasing a home. Cleaning gives you much more bang for your buck.

## Energy Efficient Appliances

Buyers are always looking for ways to save money on their future purchase, and energy efficient appliances are a great way to do this. But the trick to buying these appliances (this is especially true if you live in the house you're planning to sell) is to buy new appliances *before* the old ones break.

There are actually better months to buy appliances as well. September and October are generally when manufacturers release the latest models, so this is when old models will be discounted in order to get them off the shop floor/out of the warehouse to make room for the new ones.

If you want to double down, and wait for a potentially killer deal - January may well be your best bet. Even some of the older models will be out of stock by this time, the ones that remain will be discounted even further.

There are a few exceptions to this rule, as May is the best time to snag a bargain on refrigerators. Manufacturers want to get the new models out before summer.

Can you guess when air conditioners are at their cheapest? That's right, between October and February when the demand for them is at its lowest point.

If you're looking for a second hand appliance, you may be able to get an even better deal. Appliances are similar to cars in that they lose approximately 50% of their value as soon as they leave the store. So you can get some amazing deals on barely used, top of the line items if you check sites like Craigslist. Check out your local refurbishing center as well.

## Security features

If you're in an area populated by young couples and young families, security features are especially important. Safety and security of their kids is every parents number one concern. Having basic security systems installed in your home is an easy way to ramp up the final sale price.

On the lower end of things, roller shutters on your window might well be worth looking into.

Ironically, the alarm industry itself has long been full of sketchy characters who sell on fear or prey on the elderly. It's often tough to decide exactly how much you should spend on your alarm setup. Luckily, since the rise of the internet, and the availability of good information, it's never been easier to install your own device.

Systems will built-in smartphones apps are increasingly common these days, and you may want to spring for one with these features if you plan to sell your home anytime soon.

Avoid systems with a extremely low initial set-up cost which is then destroyed by high monthly monitoring fees. For just a few hundred dollars you can get a complete setup, with zero monthly fees

Wireless system have much greater resale value as the lack of wiring is one less thing for a new homeowner to deal with.

Additionally, It's not uncommon for homes to have CCTV cameras these days - and they are far less expensive than you think. You can install a camera yourself for as little as $100 and this could increase your overall home value by up to 5%.

One word of caution, in some states it is illegal for your camera to record a part of anyone else's property. Double check your camera angles before finalizing an installation, and consider informing your neighbors of your plan to install cameras. After all, your neighbor is someone you always want to maintain a positive relationship with.

## Your sink is the most important appliance

That's right, not your stove, not your dishwasher - your sink. If you have the extra cash, install a farmhouse sink. A study by home appraisal service Zillow found that home listed with a farmhouse sink sold for 8% above their value and 53 days sooner than similar homes that had regular sinks. These don't have to cost the Earth either, for under 200 dollars you can install one yourself, while keeping your current plumbing setup.

## The million dollar fence question

What kind of fence should you have? White picket? High enough to keep prying eyes away? The only correct answer is a freshly painted one. Get 10L of fence paint for $50 and go to town. A freshly painted fence gives off the sense that your home is well maintained and it's one less thing for a potential buyer to worry about.

## Hire a professional cleaning crew

This may be the single biggest piece of advice in this entire book. If you only have a few hundred dollars to spare on renovations, the best use of your money is to hire a full cleaning crew and let them loose in your home. Make sure absolutely everything is covered, having a spotless home will give visitors an impression of calm and relaxation.

People are visual creatures, and they want to visualize what their ideal home will look like, and believe me, no one's ideal home has dirty countertops or carpets. By presenting an image that pleases them, they're going to want to spend more money their potential new home.

## The $75 curb appeal trick

"Curb appeal" is one of those things every realtor talks about. It's vital you make sure your house gives a good first impression. An often overlooked area of this is your driveway. Luckily, you can rent a power washer from as little as $75/day and make your driveway look good as new. Go crazy with the thing and do your sidewalks (and your neighbor's), outside deck and exterior siding. As an added bonus, power washers are incredibly fun to use, and probably the closet you'll ever come to feeling like Sylvester Stallone in Rambo.

## Tapping into the lucrative Chinese home buyer market

Chinese overseas property investment has increased by a factor of 20 in the previous 10 years. Chinese citizens are projected to spend over $20 billion on property in 2017 alone, and if you live in a particularly affluent area (especially on the West coast), you may be part of their target market. But what you may not know about the Chinese is that they don't use toilet paper in their bathrooms. Instead they have a bidet (or bum-gun for those of you into less formal terminology).

What may surprise you is that installing one of these requires no additional plumbing, will save you money on toilet paper that it'll pay for itself within a year. AND, has huge appeal when selling to any portion of the Asian market, but especially the Chinese - who like to feel at home as soon as they enter a house.

**The $1 quick fix guaranteed to bring hundreds back in return**

Outlets get dirty really quick, especially white ones. But you can buy new outlet plates for $1 each, bam - brand spanking new outlet plates that give you house that extra clean touch. You can even go the extra mile and paint them to be the same color as your walls.

One addition point to make on this is the importance of consistency. Don't just replace one or two outlets, replace them all. People like consistency and regularity. Things one odd colored outlet covers can subconsciously throw off buyers without them even realizing it.

## Ditch the family photos

The old marketing adage "nobody cares about you, they only care about themselves" rings true here. People want to picture themselves in their poential new home, which also happens to be your current home. That's hard if there's 50 photos of you, your kids, your kids and Auntie Marge, your kids and Auntie Marge and her pet ferret Rollie etc.

This is where the concept of depersonalization comes in. If there's one thing 5 star hotels all have in common, it's that they are *not* personal. They are a soothing space, even somewhat neutral - a blank canvas if you will. How does this relate to your home? Well, a few family photos here and there is perfectly acceptable but try to keep them in standing photo frames rather than walled ones. Your ideal look should be a luxury hotel suite rather than someone's home. Remember, no one wants to walk into a hotel room that the maid hasn't cleaned yet. As a knock-on effect, you're going to be moving anyway so why not start the packing process earlier and save yourself a headache going forward?

## De-Clutter, De-clutter, De-clutter
This obvious tip is often overlooked by those who believe their home isn't actually cluttered. Having excess stuff just laying around makes your home look smaller than it really is, while simultaneously giving the impression of a lack of storage space.

Even if you don't want to through away some of things, at the very least put them in the attic or in the garage.

## Strategically placed mirrors
Instead of bulding a skylight or conservatory, add a few mirrors to give the impression of extra light. More maximum impact, hand these opposite a window - which gives the impressions that there are actually two windows.

## How to save thousands when hiring contractors

It cannot be stressed enough, getting the right contractor (especially for a larger job) can save you money, time and potential headaches.

The number one rule of hiring contractors is to get multiple bids for every job - at least 3. If your roof needs replacing, get 3 roofers to come and look at it. The same for if your entire home needs re-wiring, get 3 electricians in.

These 3 bids will get you 3 different answers about your needs, you can also let them know (politely) that there are other contractors looking at the job so if they're serious, they'll be willing to go above and beyond for you.

# Room-by-Room Guide to Staging Your Home

Did you know that only 10-15% of buyers can visualize your home differently than the way it looks when they walk in the door? Therefore, it's important to give them as much room for imagination as possible, and most of this revolves around keeping your house clean and removing clutter - here's a handy room by room guide to staging your house so that potential buyers get can the most out of their viewing.

# The Kitchen:

- Remove all appliances and clutter off counters. Counters should be completely clear from any non-necessary items.
- Clean all appliances. If they really look out of date, research the cost for new ones as you may get the money back - especially for worktop ones.
- Clear out the dishes. This is the perfect time to get rid of the stuff you don't want anymore - after all you'll be moving anyway. Do you really need the "world's best dad" coffee mug or the Tupperware that no longer has a lid? Donate anything you no longer need to Goodwill. Once you've done that - you can pack all the remaining dishes in preparation for your move. All you need to leave out is a single set of matching dishes in the cupboard, just so the buyer can see that someone does indeed live there right now and they're not visiting a showhome. This has the additional advantage of making your cupboard space look

more spacious when buyers open up and take a look.

- All buyers will open your fridge (I don't know why - they just will), so be sure to clean it out and of course throw out any excess food. Ideally schedule your open houses for when you are running low on supplies, because this will allow your fridge to naturally have less items in.

- The same goes for your pantry, once again donate any items you don't need and just leave a row of nicely organized items. Once again, this is to demonstrate just how spacious your cupboard and pantry space is!

- Once you've successfully decluttered and thrown out what needs to be thrown out - you can begin the staging process. This starts with a nice centerpiece on your counter. This could be an decent sized plant (like an orchid) or a big bowl of oranges or lemons (opt for the real thing). Make sure you set the dining room table as well, don't forget the unlit candles.
- If you haven't got time to bake cookies, buy some baked goods to put out for your open house. Don't forget the essential oil diffuser either, I'll explain why later in the book

# The Living Room:

- Remove the majority of the items from the mantelpiece or other shelving areas. You can leave up one or two family photos but the majority can be packed away ready for your move.

- Ditch the kid's artwork as well. I'm sure they're very talented, but you can save that for your new place.

- Hang generic artwork if you have any, if not just make sure the walls are clean.

- If the room needs to be painted, paint it,like I said before, it's one of the cheapest ways to maximize your finale sale price.

- Repair any light switches, loose curtain rods, etc. If it needs fixing - do it now. You'll have to fix it anyway, so before someone looks around your home is the best time.

- Make sure all the skirting boards and outlets are clean as well.

- Ditch any old magazines or newspapers on the table

- If you have extra furniture that takes away from your room, put it in storage. Ask your realtor if you really can't decide, they'll be able to make an informed judgment as to what buyers will like and won't like seeing. It' worth the extra expense because potential buyers are going to see your garage and spare room - so you want to keep those clean as well.

- Stick with one theme throughout your home. You don't need an Asian inspired kitchen next to your post-industrial living room for example. Your home should have a consistent and unified look. Plus this also helps you get rid of a lot of stuff

- Put a vase of flowers in the living room on open house day. You can put some finger food here as well, but I personally think the kitchen is always the best place for open house food.

# The Bathroom(s):

- Get out the travel toiletries bag, because you'll be living out of this while your home is on the market. Your bathroom needs to be spotless for the coming weeks.

- Clear away all the bottles and jars from any bath rack and within the shower itself. Don't forget the medicine cabinets either (home viewers will look)

- Repaint the bathroom as well, an easy return on investment.

- Do you have sliding shower doors? Are they sticking? If so replace the rollers, this doesn't cost a look and makes them look like new again.

- Fix any leaky faucets

- Get a new set of white towels for when you're showing the house, make your bathroom look like a hotel bathroom

- Place a single flower on the bathroom counter - just something to draw viewer's eyes in when they enter the room

# The Bedrooms:

- Remove all personal items from the dressers and bedside tables, with the exception of one, non-controversial book

- Pack away any excess clothes from your closet. If you really don't need them it's time to throw them out. Fold the rest of your clothes neatly, as if you were running a clothing store. Remember, the emptier your closet the better, give the buyer as much potential room as possible.

- Invest in new bed sheets, remember you can take these with you and it'll make the bed look much nicer for any prospective buyer. Remember - make it feel like a hotel room

- Once again, do the curtains need replacing, does the carpet need cleaning?

- Make sure your windows are clean, inside and outside.

- You can have one or two family photos but anything more will be overkill.

- If you have an additional bedroom you're currently using as a storage room, now's the time to turn it back into a bedroom again. If you were running a hotel, you wouldn't have one of the guest bedrooms as a storage closet - don't do the same in your home.

# The Exterior:

We've already covered this somewhat but it should be reiterated anyway.

• Don't neglect the outside of your home - you never get a second chance to make a good first impression
• Ensure your front door has a fresh coat of paint and that both the porch light and doorbell are fully functional - you don't want to leave potential buyers waiting outside now do you?
• Add a few pops of color to the yard, and clear out any dead plants and make sure your grass to cut
• If you have an outdoor patio or dining table, set some wine glasses on that, alternatively if it's winter and you have a firepit - get that going

## Final checks:

Take a photo of each room, is there anything out of place or any stains you haven't noticed. If not, then you can kick back and relax, maybe even pour yourself a glass of wine. The hard part of over, now you just need to let your realtor do their job and your renovations will pay for themselves in your final sale price.

## Bonus staging tip:

Create a welcome note for your buyers, introducing them to the neighborhood. Many buyers will be local so they'll already know much of the information, but it's useful for any out of town buyers who may be looking at the property. You can add handy tidbits like local attractions and niche interests that may be of use to a potential buyer.

# The #1 Most Overlooked Factor in Selling a Home

Smell is the most powerful human sense in terms of memorability. That's why certain foods always remind us of our childhood or certain events in our life.

Unfortunately, negative smells have even more of an effect than positive ones. 41 percent of real estate pros have listed "bad smells" as part of their most expensive mistakes when it came to selling a home.

Musty odors give buyers notice that there may be an underlying mold or mildew problem in the home. Both damp carpet and wet ceiling tiles are tell-tale signs of these. While you definitely need to consult a professional if you have a major mold problem, smaller issues can be dealt with by yourself. A $200 dehumidifier for example can air out any damp parts of your home.

If your open house is on a Saturday, don't cook a curry or even worse, a fish fry on the Friday night. Certain foods and spices can have a lingering smell. If you must, bake a loaf of bread in the morning, and certainly leave some cookies out if you're having an open house.

# Best Foods for an Open House

Surely the food you put out for an open house doesn't have that much of an effect? Think again.

Visuals, smells and tastes - you covered 3 senses there just by the food you're putting out. This ha a much larger psychological effect than you think.

Finger foods are the order of the day here. After all, you're not running a soup kitchen. You want something that looks nice on a table, people can take 1 or 2 without feeling a large commitment (who wants to eat a whole bowl of chili?) and ideally one or two items that fill the entire house with a warm scent to greet any buyer.

Don't go overboard on the spread either, you don't need to provide a full buffet for the entire neighborhood.

## Placement of the food

If it's nice out, lay the food out on the patio or deck outside. That way they have to go through the house (and especailly the kitchen) to get it. This also deters noisy neighbors and free-food types (think Jason Seigel's character in *I Love You, Man*)

## Chocolate Chip Cookies

The undisputed King of open house foods. They fill your kitchen with an irresistible scent that no mere mortal can resist. Everyone loves cookies and it gives a very good "welcome to your new home" vibe.

## Lemonade

Summer and lemonade, is there a better combination?
Note, if it's winter, maybe re-think the lemonade and opt for hot chocolate instead. Remeber, houses don't always sell better in the summer!

**Water**

This one is obvious but having a case of water out is useful, especially if the weather is hot. This is beneficial is buyers come with kids as well, minimizing any child-based disruption is your key to a smooth open house.

**Veggies and dip**

It's like chips and dip without the crumbs. Plus the color variety adds an extra touch of glamor to the area.

**Miniature Wrapped Candies**

Easy, no clean up required, and like cookies they're irresistible to take 1 or 2. If you're absolutely on a budget - just put a bowl of these out and you're good to go.

# Renovations that DECREASE the value of your home

## The economics of "adding value"

One of the most confusing areas when doing major renovations, is that people focus far too much on a dollar figure or percentage increase in value when examining what area to improve.

For example, during the research phase of this book, I came across multiple websites that listed adding an additional bathroom as one of the best home improvements you could make. These sites cited data that the extra bathroom could increase the value of your home up to 10%.

What they don't take into account is the cost of implementing these new rooms, which at the mid-range level can often be more than double the amount you receive in return. For example if you have a $250,000 home, and you add a bathroom to attempt to increase the value by $25,000 - what you don't know is the new bathroom is going to cost a minimum of $40,000 to install, and often a lot more. With an ROI of less than 60%, these aren't a good investment at all if you're looking at sell.

**Adding an extra bathroom - the numbers**
Based on the latest 2017 survey from Remodelling Magazine, adding an extra bathroom costs an average of whopping $43,232 and yet only has an ROI of 53.9%.

Tired of waiting for your wife (or husband) to get out of the shower? Simply add a new one! Not so fast if you want to get a decent return on investment. Studies show that this is statistically the worst investment you can make in terms of home improvement.

Even luxury bathrooms, costing an average of just over $70,000 - only represented a slightly better ROI of 55%. So not even your jacuzzi or rain shower can save you from losing money. Whirlpool baths especially are seen as one of the worst and most unnecessary waste of square footage, so even one of these in your master bathroom is not a good investment if you plan on selling your home anytime soon.

For higher ROI on bathroom related fixes, replace the tiles. It's simple, pretty boring, and won't win you any design plaudits, but it is something that potential buyers will appreciate.

**Making a giant master bedroom.**
One of the biggest myths is that everyone wants a giant master bedroom. More people are concerned with having more bedrooms, even if they don't currently have the family to use them. Many buyers think ahead while buying a house, and

space for future family members plans heavily into this.

The same goes with removing closet space to extend the master bathroom, everyone needs closet space - but not everyone needs a huge bathroom. It's a matter of making your home appeal to the biggest possible market

## Invisible improvements

Peaceful living may require a brand new plumbing system and HVAC (Heating, Ventilation and Air Conditioning) unit, but home buying is still very much a visual experience. Potential buyers are going to be far more enthused by a clean kitchen with sparkling countertops (even if they're 15 years old) than by a blanket statement of "we replaced the wiring last year." Home buyers often just expect the behind-the-scenes stuff like wiring and plumbing to be in full working order, and aren't willing to pay a premium just because you did it recently.

Visible and cosmetic improvements are what make buyers emotionally attached to a property, and emotional attachment is the reason people overpay for things. After all, when was the last time someone was "enamored" by brand new wiring?

## Remodelling your home office

Despite the rise in working from home, and desktop entrepreneurs - not everyone wants a dedicated office space in their home. In an age where square footage matters more than anything, a large home office is seen as wasteful. So before you go tearing down any walls, consider that the space could be much better put to use by adding another bedroom.

## An external generator

Unless you live in a state where power outages are frequent, many buyers see this as wasteful, especially the frugal ones who are constantly worried about their utility bills. While you may see a handy backup solution, others see additional maintenance costs for something that may not even use once a year.

**Trying to outgrow your area**

Let's face it, no one wants a $400,000 home in a street surrounded by $250,000 homes. For one it draws extra attention to you and could well be a security risk. Secondly, buyers judge the quality of the neighborhood just as much as the quality of the house. Don't build an enormous extension, your money is better off spent elsewhere.

This also applies to the general standard of furnishing in your home. Think back to the consistency point made earlier in the book. If you have a top of the line, newly renovated $50,000 kitchen, but a bathroom that looks like it is stuck in a time warp from 1972 - this puts off potential buyers. You may see a beautiful kitchen, but they may see a $20,000 bathroom renovation project, that they neither have the time nor the money to worry about. If you have a large wad of cash burning a hole in your pocket and you have decided to make major renovations, it's better to evenly spread your money around than just focus on making one room stand out above the rest.

As a general guideline, your home value should not be anything more than 20% higher than the rest of your neighborhood, anything more than this can have an adverse effect.

# It's Time to Sell

You've done the hard work, now it's time to reap your rewards with the sale. Check out these handy tips to put you on the right path.

## Get the right agent

Too often, people go for an agent through referral from a friend or family member. However, agents often specialize in certain price ranges or certain areas. If your agent did a great job on your sister-in-law's 2 bed apartment, she might not be the best choice for your 5 bed converted farmhouse.

Go to open houses in your area and your projected price range, get a feel for the agent and see if he or she is someone you'd want to work with. Open houses are as much a chance for agents to get new clients as they are for selling a house. Finding the right agent is vital and too often, money is left on the table by those who settle for the first agent they come across.

## The Important of Timing

Timing your sale can often lead to up to a 20% increase in overall value. So if houses in your area aren't selling for the price you had in mind, it's worth it to hold off for a few months or even up to 2 years to get the figure you want. The other factor to note is what time of year you should list your house. Conventional wisdom has always said that spring and summer is the best time to sell - but that may not always be true. You see, because everyone knows this, there's a lot more competition during these months, and thus it may be harder for you to achieve your goal sale price.

Looking at the numbers, houses listed in winter (between December 21 and March 21) are more likely to sell within 6 months, spend 6 days less on the market and fetch a final sale price that's 1.2%

*higher* than the equivalent home listed in any other season.

The reasoning for this is that serious home buyers will still be looking during the winter months, and these will be the ones more likely to make you the offer you want on your home.

# Things that you should mention in your ad

You may not think any of these matter when determining your home value, but they do. If any of these tick the boxes of your area, you should absolutely mention them to draw in niche buyers.

### Proximity to sporting venues

Live a 15 minute drive away from MetLife stadium or just down the road from The American Airlines Arena? Write this down in your ad. Season ticket holders will go crazy for a location like this. One of the most annoying things about going to sports game is the potentially long drive to get there, so if you can show that the long drive no longer exists, or even better if you have public transit access, then you're onto a winner.

And non sporting fans? They won't really care, but it won't have a negative effect with them.

## Proximity to Starbucks

Is there a Starbucks just down the street? People love the idea (even if they never go once they move in) of being able to sit outside with friends and family and enjoy a cup of their favorite caffeinated concoction. Starbucks also has a connotation with the area being affluent or "up and coming". So, if you have one near you, especially within walking distance - don't hesitate to let buyers or your realtor know.

## Military Bases

Homes near army bases go for up to $50,000 more than the national median house price, and those near Navy, Marine and Coast Guard bases can be up to $90,000 more. Military members often don't have the luxury of being able to shop around when being assigned to a new base, and as such will likely overpay for a house in a convenient location moreso than other buyers.

## Marijuana

Regardless of your personal views, the marijuana industry is one of the fastest growing in the entire countries. If you live in a recreational state, that's Alaska, Colorado, Maine, Massachusetts, Nevada, Oregon and Washington, (plus California from January 2018) for those of you keeping tabs - then your home price could be significantly impacted by the industry. Entrepreneurs, medical tourists and those looking to work in the industry are flocking towards these areas.

# 9 Secrets your realtor won't tell you

1.    If you get a last minute call to view, let them.

It may seem counterintuitive to let someone view your non-pristine home, but it's worth it. Last minute viewers are impulsive types, they might take a quick look around your house and make you an offer right there and then.

2.    Never turn away a lowball offer

You're more likely to get a positive response by negotiating with someone who's already made an offer on your place than you are with a new prospect. Maybe these prospects had poor information regarding prices in the area, or maybe they were just trying their luck (anyone who has done any form of negotiating has done this at least once in their life).

3.   Going with the agent who promises you the highest selling price, especially if it's way higher than everyone else.

There are always one or two agents who try this. It's the exact opposite situation to the previous issue. All they're doing with this tactic is trying to win your business. If you go with them, despite knowing better, your house is guaranteed to sit on the market, unsold, for a lot longer.

As this number increases, people start to speculate just why the house has been on the market for so long. There *must* be something wrong with it, and any offers that do come in are certain to be lowball ones.

Real estate investor and coach Phil Pustejovsky calls this the "kiss of death" - on one property alone this can cost you tens of thousands of dollars, and if you're a full-time investor that can add up to over 6 figures if you continue to make bad deals.

4.   You can negotiate commissions

If you and your buyer are a few thousand apart, approach both of your realtors and see if they'll both reduce their commissions in order to get the deal done. It won't work every time, but it's always worth a shot.

5.   Ask about their history, especially their recent history

Even though an agent might have had their license for years, they're only worth what they've done lately. For example, a family friend with 20 years in the business might not have sold a house within the past 3 years. Always ask a prospective agent about their recent dealings.

6. Sellers should guide buyers through their home to give a personal touch to the process.

Absolutely not, if you are glued to the side of a prospect, you make them uneasy and feel like they're intruding in *your* home, not viewing what could potentially be *their* home. It's probably best if you aren't there for a viewing, and especially for an open house.

7. You should bide your time when you receive an offer, because it gives you more negotiating leverage.

In sales, delay is decay. Mood swings happen, people sour on offers. You don't benefit from delaying the transaction. If the offer is too low, negotiate - but negotiate right away.

8. Eventually someone will offer the price you wanted

This ties in with point number 3. If you selected an agent who listed at the highest price, and your property sits on the market for more than 30, 60 or even 90 days - buyers will notice this. They question what's wrong with the home, and the only offers you do get will be the lowball ones.

9.  You shouldn't hire an agent with lots of other clients because they'll be too busy to focus on selling your home

There's a reason they have a lot of clients, it's because they're good. It's the same reason why popular restaurants are always busy, and the best cosmetic surgeons have month-long wait lists. These realtors have top quality assistants to help them with things like research and scheduling, they just focus on getting the best results for their clients.

# And the 1, undisputed truth?

**You need a realtor to get the best value for your home**

There's no substitute for experience, and selling a home is not something you become an expert in overnight. Yes, you'll save on commissions, but what use is that if you sell for 10 or 15% below market value? A study by the National Association of Realtors found the the average For Sale by Owner (FSBO) home sold for $185,000, whereas the average realtor sold home sold for $245,000 - that's a difference of a huge **$60,000**!

So even when you take out the average 6% commission for the agent, you're still leaving almost $50,000 on the table if you elect to sell your home yourself. I don't know about you, but to me that's not exactly the smartest financial decision.

Sellers aren't always the best judges of value, especially if it's a home you've lived in for a long time. More often than not, you will end up netting more by selling your home through a realtor, even after their commission is taken out.

Thanks to the internet, it's never been easier to get the best realtor for your home, websites such as http://www.realtrends.com/ allow you to search in your area for the realtor who has got the best results for their clients in terms of homes sold by dollar amount.

Remember, even an average realtor sells 11 homes a year, with the top ones coming out at around 35 sales per year. Don't leave a big financial decision up to chance by trying to do it all on your own just to save a few thousand on commissions - it's not worth it

# How to Negotiate Your Home Sale Like a Pro

More often than not, buyers who get less than they wanted for their home, do so not because they didn't make the right renovations, but because they're poor negotiators. By taking the time to learn some basic (yet highly effective) negotiation techniques, you put yourself is a much better position.

1.   Remove all emotion from the deal

This may be hard if it's a home that's been in your family for over a hundred years. But guess what, when it comes to crunch time, your buyer doesn't care. Think of this like a simple business transaction, like you're selling staplers or juice boxes.

Remeber this: Successful real estate investors make a lot of their money buying from emotional sellers.

2.   Establish a backup plan

In the real estate industry, this is known as a BATNA (best alternative to a negotiated agreement). This is when you decide your plan If you can't reach your desired amount. Maybe it's to hold onto the house for another year, or to rent it out in the meantime - but having a plan like this means you are less likely to accept a number that was below your target.

3.   Really consider your first offer

Your first offer is likely to be the best one, so the first offer you receive is a good gauge of the market in general. This doesn't mean you have to sell at that price, but is does suggest that they want your house, and are willing to do what it takes to get it.

4.  Counter it at your list price

What separates the amateurs from the pros when it comes to negotiation is countering. Often a buyer's offer will be low enough that the seller counters with an offer at below the list price. This is done as people naturally want to appear friendly, amiable or willing to compromise. Unfortunately, all these does is cost you, the seller, money.

Some buyers will be surprised by this, and will walk way - but by doing this you also avoid timewasters who are just trying to look for a bargain.

5.  Create a bidding war

Bidding wars are fantastic as it allows buyers to compete against each other and push up the selling price. The easiest way to do this is to not entertain any offers at an open house, or before a certain date. For example, you put your house on the market and decide to tell you agent to not receive any offers for the first week. Often times, you may only get one offer using this strategy, but the offer will be higher than if you had just accepted all offers at the beginning.

Note: Creating a bidding war is not the same as fabricating one. Never tell the buyer there's another offer if there isn't one - it's easy for them to find out and if they call you out on it, you've lost a sale, plus your reputation takes a hit.

6.   Don't give the buyer any leverage

For example, if they ask why you're selling, simply say you decided to move to a bigger property. They don't need to know you're behind on mortgage payments, or are moving halfway across the country - both of which signal that you need to get the transaction done quickly and would be easy to lowball.

# Tips for buying a home - so you maximize profit down the line

We've previously covered emotion in buying and selling, and how it can cost you a good deal. But this is no more true on when buying a home. This especially applies to your first home, but is still very much relevant to any home you buy within the first 10 years of your real estate journey.

Why the first 10 years? This is the period of time before you experience the benefits of long-term investing with things such as compound interest. Your overall cash flow is lower, and your margin for error is thinner. Top South Carolina real estate investor Chad Carson, a man who started his journey with just $1,000 in his pocket says

"Particularly, in your first 10 years, if you make mistakes of buying emotionally on your residence as opposed to buying in a very calculated manner by making your residence a house-hack or a live-and-flip, or just renting and investing that somewhere else, the magnitude of that mistake is huge 20 to 30 years from now.

"It's like $700,000, [or] a million-dollar difference, for somebody 20 to 30 years later who made the choice to make their first home a nice home, a great neighborhood, and being in the top high school as opposed to making a decision to treat your home like an investment or just rent. It's a major, major difference."

# How to beat the competition when buying your dream home

Chances are, you won't be the *only* ones in a good home buying position after reading this book. If you find a good deal on the market, there will be competition, so you'll have to place yourself in a position where your offer is the one the seller goes with. Now obviously, you want to do that in a way that doesn't involve spending drastically more money, and suddenly making a good deal into a bad one. Here are a number of ways you can appear like the most desirable candidate to any seller.

1.   Ensure your finances are a fortress of stability

Just being pre-approved for a mortgage doesn't cut it any more, that's entry level stuff. In the internet age, it's never been so easy to get a pre-approval letter, and sellers are getting smart to this. If you want to stand out, then work with a reliable local mortgage lender or endorsed local provider (ELP) and have them give you the seal of approval

2.   Show them you're serious
If you haven't heard of earnest money before, now's the time to learn. Earnest money is an amount you pledge as a deposit to the buyer to show them your true intentions of buying the home. Often this will be 1-2% of the total purchase price, but you can higher if there is competition. This doesn't mean you pay more for the house, as the money will be applied to your down payment - but by offering this up front, it puts you a step ahead of the competition. This also

3. Add a personal touch to the process

Consider submitting your offer in the form of a handwritten letter. This old-timey trick can put the seller at ease, and make a business transaction into a less formal event. You'll still need to be competitive with your offer, but if it's down to you and another buyer - this little letter may well swing things in your favor.

# How to Get The Most Money for Your Home - Even if You Have a Deadline to Sell by

In an ideal world, home sales would be a stress-free, blissful process - but we don't live in an ideal world, we live in the real world. People get new jobs and have to move to a new city, or parents get sick and require 24/7 care. This speeds up the sale process from one that takes months to something you have to finish within weeks. Whatever the reason, there are very few situations that are more stressful than having to sell a home quickly. Luckily, there are a number of ways to get the most for your home in situations like this.

1. List use house using a conservative price estimate.

This isn't the time to shoot for the moon, listing you house on the lower end of the price spectrum is likely to encourage multiple offers.

2. Set a deadline for offers

Use the principle of scarcity to encourage offers as well. People always want what they can't have, so setting a deadline, even if it's just 1 or 2 weeks after the house goes on the market, can net you multiple offers if buyers think they only have a limited window to get in on the deal.

3. Don't indicate you need to sell quickly

Following on from point 2, even though there's a deadline, you don't need to give a reason for one. You may be panicking inside, but your buyer doesn't need to know that. It's vital you keep a cool head during the selling process, and this can be tough if you are selling for emotional reasons (e.g. a death in the family)

4.  Hire a Professional Stager

If time is tight, and renovations are out of the questions - consider hiring a professional home stager. A report by the National Assocation of Realtors (NAR) showed that 81% of buyers felt that staging helped them imagine the property they were viewing as a future home. Staged home also sell quicker than non-staged ones, and in some states the difference is staggering. In Oregon for example, pre-staged homes sold a huge 7 times faster than non-staged ones and in California the rate was 5 times faster.

Staging costs vary from state-to-state, but the national median tends to run around $600. Your real estate agent will have staging contacts, so it's best to use them as a resource if your time is limited.

## 5.   Put away your cellphone camera

The vast majority of buyers now do research online before viewing a home. Poor quality photos that don't truly show off your home are guaranteed to lose you money when it comes to crunch time. So as tempting as it may be to whip out your iPhone and start snapping away, leave it to a pro. You don't even have to hire a pro to do this, even just getting a friend with a keen interest in photography and a knowledge of angles and lighting is enough. Even taking pictures in the right time of day with a proper camera is infinitely better than running around the house with any old cellphone camera.

## 6.   Be flexible about viewing times

If you have serious time constraints, then you need to maximize what little time you do have to show your property. I advise scheduling viewing at all times of the day, even traditionally non-appealing times like evenings. This will involve keeping your home extremely clean at all time, in the case of a short-notice viewing. Remember, when you have buyers looking around - give them space

If you have pets, any signs of them should not be apparent in the home. Paraphernalia like dog bowls or cat litter boxes should be cleared away, and if you can help it - don't give any signs that pets are in the home. This isn't because your viewers aren't animal lovers, or don't have pets of their own, but it'll help them envisions their dream home easier.

## 7.   Do the extra promotion yourself

If you're constrained by time, you're going to have to get creative if you want to maximize your return.

Don't just leave the marketing element up to your agent. Get on social media, tell family and friends about the house. You never know which friend-of-a-friend-of-a-friend needs a house just like yours. If you're part of a homeowners association, send your listing to their email list and you can get your neighbors to help advertise for you.

8. Use an essential oil diffuser to give a great first impression

If you don't have time to bake cookies 4 times a day (and who does?) to get that freshly baked smell wafting through the home, you can use an essential oil diffuser to get the same effect. You can put one near the door with a neutral scent like lavender or rosemary to gives a great first impression when a potential buyer walks through the door. Consider setting some fresh flowers out as well, this is a powerful visual tool that puts buyers in the right mood as soon as they walk in your door.

8.5 Use a drop of vanilla in a warmed oven to replicate the smell of freshly baked cookies

An old realtor hack, if you don't have time to bake, just do the above and your house will smell like freshly baked cookies!

9.   Avoid guaranteed sales programs

Have you ever seen those ads from realtors that say "If you don't sell your home within 30 days, we'll buy it". All these people do is list your home at a price no one is willing to pay, then give you a lowball offer at the end of the 30 day period. Causing you to take a massive loss.

10.  List your home on a Thursday or Friday

Doing this will put your fresh in the minds of buyers and agents when they're planning their weekend viewings. A study by real estate website Redfin found that homes listed on a Friday sold for an average of $2,800 higher than homes listed on a Sunday.

# Conclusion

So there we have it, cheap, creative ways, and even free ways that you can maximize the value of your home. Applying just a few of these to your home sale can net profits of 5, 10 or even 20% higher than you would have received without them.

Now compound those profits over multiple homes and we're potentially talking about hundreds of thousands of dollars - not bad for a few coats of paint, or a smart decision on which day of the week you list your home!

I hope you've learned a lot in this book and you can use the tips in your own home sale. Selling a home can be stressful, especially if this is your first go around the block, but when armed with what you've learned in this book, you can be confident about netting the highest possible sale price for you and your family.

Finally, if you've enjoyed this book I'd really appreciate if you went took just 2 minutes to leave it a review on Amazon.

www.ingramcontent.com/pod-product-compliance
Lightning Source LLC
Chambersburg PA
CBHW071502210326
41597CB00018B/2665